THE TRUE STORY OF IDA JOHNSON

Sharon Riis

The Women's Press
Toronto

Printed and Bound by
Charters Publishing Company Limited,
Brampton, Ontario, Canada
Typeset at The Women's Press in co-operation with
The Coach House Press
Cover Design by Pat Bourque

Born 15.10.47

Box 6
Longview
Alberta
Canada

to the careful reader

The truth of the matter is: there is none.

Why didn't you burn, Ida?

I was outside.

Outside? It was four a.m. What were you doing outside girl?

Well. I thought I heard someone.

Did Derek hear anything?

No. He was sleeping.

Was anyone there then?

I didn't see anyone but...

But?

Well I really think somebody *was* there.

Who?

I don't know. But you see I went out to look I was so sure. That's when it blew up.

The trailer.

Yeah. Everything.

What did you do?

Nothing. The whole town was there before I even moved.

How did you feel?

I was cold.

Haneck wheeled his 2-ton into the Claresholm Esso more out of habit than hunger. *Eats Full Co rse Meals*, resplendent in red neon, marked the beginning of the end of his Kimberley-Calgary fruit run. He had to stop, if only for coffee and an oil check, or his timing would be off. On those rare occasions when experience didn't correspond precisely to expectation he panicked and feared some consequence or other for days. He'd already made one mistake that morning and wasn't about to compound the error. Coming down through the Crow's Nest Pass, comfortable in the warmth of the cab with his own good company, Haneck thought he saw the slight still figure of a man in an enormous greatcoat by the side of the road. Must've dozed off, he thought, startled. He'd never done that in a lifetime of trucking. But he hadn't met another driver for hours. There's nothing out there, he reasoned. "No sense in it," he said aloud to the green lights on the dash maybe, or the plush dice that danced from the rear-view mirror. But the image stayed; and thinking of the cold and the threatening snow, bothered by the tightness in his chest, he turned the truck around.

"A goddamned kid!" he exclaimed when the lights caught hold of the body and made it real. The blood was pounding in back of his ears and his head hurt. Haneck, just turned sixty-three, had never actually seen a dead person before. When the body, its back to the highway, did a slow ninety degree turn to stare him square in the face, Haneck nearly shit his pants. When the body grinned "Mornin' " at him, Haneck very nearly clubbed it to death.

"What're you doing out here boy? What in hell...?!"

"Waiting for you," the boy said, and Haneck was silent and afraid, really *afraid*, that he knew nothing.

The boy released him. "Waiting for a lift," he corrected. "Thanks for stopping."

"Get in," Haneck told him. "It's bloody cold." Then, fifty miles on: "Where you heading?"

"East."

Not exactly a raving conversationalist, thought Haneck. "What's your name?" he ventured.

"Luke," said the boy and laughed perversely enough to check the old man's curiosity for good.

It was six a.m. They both went into the cafe; Haneck motioned for coffee; neither said a word. The mechanic from Al's Service Station and two CPR freight drivers were inside waiting for their ham and eggs. Ida brought the coffee and went back to her position against the pop cooler where she had left a Players burning. Nobody said a word. You could hear the cook banging around out back and the ham frying. It was warm there and smelled like home. Ida nodded at Haneck and studied the odd-looking youth from out the corner of her eye. Who's this black-eyed bum? she wondered, defensive for some reason. But she noted the sheepskin coat with approval. It must've cost some, she thought. He looked like a foreigner, or a film cowboy even. That impressed her too but she still didn't like the way his eyes burned.

Haneck pulled out a quarter and said, "You ready?"

"I'm staying," said Luke.

Haneck hid his relief, grunted, put the quarter under his saucer and left.

Ida came over and pocketed the money without looking up. He's hard, she thought. She was sure about that. Hard.

*

She's gone to fat, thought Luke. Her uniform was white and stiffly starched. It came halfway down her calf though the buttons strained against her midriff. An attempt had been made to order her dull heavy hair into a bun. Her eyes were smudged with mauve shadow.

I'll tell him to piss off in a minute if he doesn't stop staring, she thought, and smoothed her hair back. What cruddy manners.

A tired woman near forty came in wearing a man's overcoat and white nursing shoes. Everybody looked up.

"Hi Shirl," said Ida.

"Morning honey," said Shirl. The mechanic blew her a kiss.

"You're kind of slow to move today ain't you Bob?" she teased.

Shirl usually took the night shift. She had six kids and an old man who wanted his meat and potatoes on time. About one week out of ten her unmarried sister from Maple Creek would come to stay and give Shirl something of a rest. Ida would change shifts around because she liked Shirl and it was only right.

"Just waiting for you sweetheart. Couldn't get through the morning without seeing your smiling face."

"Hah!" laughed Shirl, "You got Ida here to look at so don't give me that!"

"Yeah, Ida's got a nice ass but she don't smile on a man. Always looks like she's been drinking sour milk by the pailful!"

"Ah shut your yap," mumbled Ida.

"See?!" said Bob. Everybody laughed but the boy in the coat. Even Ida had to smile.

"I'll make more coffee before I go off," said Ida. She really did like Shirl.

"Thanks. I'll get my apron." But she motioned for Ida to follow her into the kitchen.

"Morning Mr. Fung," she called. The old Chinaman peeked out from behind a stack of utensils and bowed. He looked about nine hundred years old according to Ida and he gave her the creeps. He didn't have any friends or a TV or anything and never left the cafe that she knew of (though Shirl once told her that long ago he had gone to Hong Kong for a bride but she died on the boat coming back); he slept on a grotty little cot right in the back there by the toilet. Bride or no bride Ida thought he was crazy and wouldn't go near him; she made him leave her pay in an envelope in the till every Friday. She could never figure out why Shirl always acted like he was her favourite uncle or something.

"So who's the beauty queen?" Shirl whispered.

"Huh?"

"Pretty boy out there! Who is he? He's sure been giving you the magic stare honey."

"I don't know. How am I supposed to know? He came in with Haneck this morning."

"Boy oh boy I wouldn't mind a little of that. Hey? Hey! Come on, get the lead out girl!" And she gave Ida a slap on the ass and a wink with her smile and was gone.

"You're a fruitcake Henderson!" Ida yelled after her. But she took another look at the cowboy on her way to the coffee urns.

Bob paid for his breakfast and left. Ida noticed he didn't leave any tip though he always left Shirl a nickle. The other two had finished eating and were lighting up some butts. It was a quarter to seven. Shirl was printing *Today's Specials* on a piece of cardboard. Ida set about making more coffee. She saw that the boy was sweating; saw him take off his coat and shake so bad with cold that he had to put it back on. She watched him cross to the jukebox. Like a dancer, she thought. He pushed for *San Quentin*, *Jackson*, and *Darlin' Companion* and nearly passed out leaning there against the machine. He had to laugh then, at his lack of control. It was a strange new pose. He felt terribly, terribly old. There's a chance, he thought. I've a chance to be young. Dear Ida, dear dear Ida.

*

14

Longview escapes the prairie by twenty miles and the mountains by twenty-five. It alters the minds of passers-through like an empty but unforgettable dream of nothing in particular. But nobody ever does pass through so what does that matter? The inhabitants number anywhere from a hundred to a hundred and twenty depending on the season and the inclination of a very few to leave. Almost everybody stays.

It's a children's paradise but time eats children.

I've been with you from the beginning Ida though when I came into the cafe it was the first you'd seen of me in a long long while. It was six in the morning and I stopped with the trucker who'd picked me up on the old Kimberley-Calgary trail. A less astute onlooker might feel sorry for you Ida, might think you were a local girl tied somehow, forever, to that small armpit of a no-town where I found you working as a waitress. But I knew you'd made it in your own particular way. You'd dismissed your past, most of it; the future was of no concern at all. There were no loose ends for you. Christ girl, you amaze even me.

You didn't look so good but then your shift was almost over. You recognized me. I know you don't think you did but I saw the glaze lift for a moment when you brought the coffee. Your eyes are nice without the glaze but then that's like saying your skin is clear without the blemishes: it just wouldn't be you would it? Still, you've got awfully good legs. But I don't have to tell you that.

I put a quarter in the box and played three Johnny Cash numbers thinking it might wake you up. You felt sure I was from the city then and that amused you. You were too tired to be interested by it.

Fucking right I recognized you. How slow do you think I am sweetheart? How far out of touch or deep into the hum or over the hill or off into the sunset? Luke, eh? Never really did know how to fake it did you?

Every now and then somebody raises a finger to the claustrophobia of fate and wins. Lucy George was one. The Indian Affairs man, Cliff McKay, took her out of the Reservation School and put her into grade four at Longview Elementary when she was seven. After two months she had the good sense to return home though everyone mumbled "just like an Indian" and took personal offence at her ingratitude. She disappeared from the Reserve itself a couple of years later and nobody gave her another thought except Ida.

Can I buy you a coffee?

Are you kidding?

I'd like to talk to someone.

You can buy me breakfast. Got any money?

Yes.

You want something?

Another coffee.

Seven miles back up the Highwood River there's an old graveyard with four maybe five graves in it. It sits on a small rise in the middle of the range to the left of the river. Nobody knows who's buried there but everyone has their own idea. Some say it's the family of an early rancher hit hard by the smallpox and others claim it to be the doings of those niggers on the Reserve.

Ida wasn't the least surprised when the kid asked her to sit and have coffee. In fact she'd already decided to. It might be worth something. That coat cost. She was no hooker or anything but if a guy wanted to give her ten bucks she wouldn't say no. But god she felt nervous. It bothered her. She couldn't remember the last time she felt her stomach flap around like that.

"What's your name?" she asked.

"Luke."

"I'm Ida." She thought maybe she should shake his hand or something but she didn't. Why didn't he say anything? Take a good look whydontcha? she felt like saying but instead: "OK Shirl! The works! And another coffee for the cowboy here."

Shirl was smiling and winking and carrying on like she was crazy from across the room; Ida nearly got up and slugged her for it. Luke smiled then and that made Ida want to cry. Pull yourself together Johnson, she told herself, this guy's a piece of cake.

Lucy was born to Mary and Henry George on October 15, 1950. She'd been around a lot longer than that of course but nobody knew and she wasn't the sort who'd tell. Henry died the following winter from an unfortunate bout with bad whiskey but Mary was enough family for anyone with her gummy smile and greasy bulk and her big love for Lucy.

Luke still said nothing. Ida thought maybe she better make some conversation before they both fell asleep. "Hey!" she said, "Don't I know you from some place?" and Luke coughed a full cup of coffee into his lap.

"Well Jesus," said Ida, concerned. There was a great commotion on the part of Shirl who ran over with an old dish rag to mop up and cluck in the pretty boy's ear. "You okay now honey?" she asked, sliding him another cup.

"Thanks," he said. "I'm fine."

"Right," said Ida. "Where were we?"

"You thought you might know me from some place."

"Yeah."

"What place?"

"I don't know. Anyplace. Around. Who cares? Right, sweetheart? Hey. What's your angle anyways?"

"I need to talk to someone. Tell me about yourself. Everything. Beginning to end. That's all. Will you?"

"Me?"

Luke nodded.

"Hell, what's it worth?" she asked.

"Call your price," he said.

"Jesus. I'll talk your ear off for twenty."

"You're on. But I want the truth."

"Sure thing honey." Whatever gets you off, she thought.

*

It's my first memory this. I must've been four. We were all up fishing my Dad and brother mostly and Mom with the lunch and her embroidery. I got to hold the rod for awhile and there's a picture somewhere of me doing it. It was hot I remember though the trees had turned. I was hunting around for things and well I did see this garter snake really small and I wasn't afraid or anything. I thought it would scare my Mom if I could catch it and I followed it through the long grass up a small hill actually where I found some very neat piles of rocks. I always thought at that time that I was the first to be anywhere when I was by myself or even to do anything but I knew with those rocks that someone had been ahead of me there. The scream could be heard all the way back to the Hindle ranch. It lasted a full minute and scared the pants off me it wasn't till later I understood it was actually me screaming. I must've fallen six feet into that hole. Once the noise passed it wasn't so bad there and I started looking around. The bones didn't scare me—I'd seen cow skulls before for instance—but I didn't like the dark so I tried moving the thing into the light from the hole but it began to whimper and when I dropped it at that it crumbled away to nothing. Like chalk I thought. I wasn't so much afraid as terrible sad and I started to cry but something warm and cold both came out of the dark around me close like a friend and I was glad. When Mr. Hindle and my Dad found me they were more mad than anything that I hadn't called out when I heard them yelling for me but actually I didn't hear them though they never thought to believe me.

Ida's parents appeared to be simple unassuming people; but none are that. They were excessively secretive: Ole fundamentally so, Esther more than likely through marriage and the consequent adaption of her personality to that of her keeper. Her essential manner, hidden away in some private cupboard of memory and fantasy for none to see, became secretive. Her face was dead though neither wooden nor gloomy. It held no clues.

Ole exposed himself perhaps twice a year. An oppressive blackness would well up and smear his face with rage. Nothing followed. No verbal or physical violence ever shook the household. The blackness just drained away.

Ida followed Chuck by six years, too late for connection to be made. He ignored her out of habit, and Ida soon learned from the rest to make her business her own. They were four worlds in contained orbit around the secret that had no name. Silence, soothed with occasional gentle interaction, prevailed.

When I was two I started Sunday School and so on and so forth for many years. I went because that's what kids did on Sunday mornings and because I won everything for attendance and knowing my verses and being fairly polite. I won plaques. "Blessed are the meek for they shall inherit the earth" is one I still have somewhere. I really got to know Jesus, you know? When I was eight some kids who I won't name and me headed out for the Bar W ranch where we knew they had a few sheep but the full grown ones were truly enormous so we got a hold of this lamb and held it good so we could hit it with rocks. In general we made a mess of it and it took a long time before it was dead and some of the kids got sick but I had enough smarts to bring matches and got everyone organized into getting wood and whatnot and we had some largish rocks so as to build an altar but the burning wool stunk so bad we couldn't finish with it so we left. It was time to get home anyway. I ripped my arm along some barbed wire as in explanation of the blood for my mother.

Lucy was the best friend I ever had though it didn't last long to be sure since she was around such a short time. My mother didn't like her much being an Indian and all but wouldn't say so openly and I just ignored what wasn't said as I liked Lucy so. I was older than her of course but she taught me a lot just the same. That first day she came to the school she was skinny and dirty like you wouldn't believe and everyone just stared. Miss Bird asked if she had lice right out loud and everybody laughed and laughed including myself but old Lucy just smiled and said "No, actually. Do you?" She got the strap for it alright but nobody ever laughed at her again.

The shift in perspective that took God out of fashion did nothing to destroy the illusory stuff from which he was made; it merely dispersed the power that had been his alone. When Lucy asked Ida if she believed in Fate she said "You mean like in horoscopes? Sure, why not?" It was then (Fall '57) that Lucy presented Ida with the first in a series of personal statements that she hoped might redress her friend's imbalance. Lucy, it goes without saying, was a purist. She had a lot to learn.

In the beginning was not the word but was will.
Out of the will comes a will that is me.
Out of me comes the world.
More:
Out of me comes the will.
I am the beginning and the end.

My Aunt Hazel and Uncle Charles who were in fact not directly so related to me at all but were my godparents had been married twenty-five years so there was to be a big celebration at their place which was just six or seven houses up the road. Everybody was coming from Saskatchewan and even some relative or other from B.C. My own Grandma and Grandpa on my mother's side from south of Swift Current came and a lot of kids that were my first and second cousins so I was happy as anybody. To look at a photo of my Grandpa you'd think he was real stern and fierce but in fact he just told funny stories all the time and gave me lifesavers to suck on. My Grandma was big and fat and I think truly jolly though how can a person tell? She told me she'd never kissed Grandpa until they were engaged. She knew a million hymns for playing on the organ. My Mom and her would talk with low voices in the kitchen whenever she came. I don't know what about. She didn't like Catholics and sometimes I was afraid of meeting one in the gully though I can tell you now I never did.

Anyway the party went off without a hitch except that the ornamental icing on the cake was so hard it couldn't be cut through and had to be lifted off before anybody could get a piece. That spoiled some of the pictures and made Aunt Hazel get all shrill. There was enough food to feed an army as the saying goes. I don't know who did the dishes. Us kids played scrub in the field behind the house and my brother and a couple of older kids went riding around in Stella's boyfriend's new convertible that had a radio. Stella was Hazel and Charles' girl who had an office job in Calgary and wore mascara and everything. My Mom and all the other ladies talked and talked about whoever they knew from before in the olden days with their voices low as always. The men stood hunched together and played horseshoes or told stories which they all laughed at like they were the funniest things they'd ever heard. When it was getting dark all the men started to drink the beer that had been in the washtub all day and the rye that was warm of course. Some of the ladies too, even my Mom though one drink lasted her the whole night and I know she didn't like even that one though it was such a special occasion. Uncle Charles found an extension cord and brought out their record player so everyone could dance. The little kids got put to bed in the house and I had to put my sweater on. My brother Chuck sat in the back seat of Grandpa's Dodge all night with Jenny Erikson who was twelve and from Sask and ran the battery dead by playing the radio all the time. I know he had some beer because of the way his breath smelled when he told me to get lost.

The music started. It was *Dance of the Finland Woods* and my Dad's face was bright and shining. I'd never seen him so happy. He danced and danced. He was King of the dancing and all the ladies liked to whirl round and round with him he was so light on his feet and so strong at the same time. Fox Trot. Mazurka. Waltz. Schottische. Round and round. He even danced with me and I was never so happy. My Mom's mouth got tighter and tighter the more he danced even though he danced a lot with her. She would try to get even by being mean to me telling me I should be in bed and whatnot but I just took off and kept on the other side of the yard with Lloyd who was about my age and his little sister Gudrun. Eventually it was coffee time again and more lunch was put out so everyone knew it was time to go home. Nobody wanted to fiddle around with Grandpa's battery so we walked. My mother told Chuck it was impolite to sit like that in the car all night. The next day and the day after my Mom was very quiet and couldn't say anything nice even though my Grandma and Grandpa were staying with us.

*

My Mom would pack me a lunch on Saturdays and Lucy and I would head through the gully looking for something we hadn't found before. Mom never said nothing but the lunch got bigger each time we went out so I knew she was thinking of Lucy in a good way though god knows she'd never say. I expect she was glad I had a friend even if she was Reserve. Before Lucy came I played by myself mostly. I didn't mind but my Mom not to mention Chuck would make me cry sometimes asking why nobody ever called for me. I didn't know. It was like another world out there in the gully with Lucy. We were pirates and birds, dope smugglers and settlers, cougars and soldiers and ships and cowboys and queens and coyotes and bullfighters and bushes and stars...And I don't know what all. When we'd come home it would be dark and everything moved like a dream. It was the same with school. I hated it. It had nothing to do with me. I hated it but I had to go as I was only ten.

Lucy told me "I killed God" she said and laughed whereas I took it very seriously as for instance she'd never lied to me before that I knew of so I asked her how she'd done it and she said she sat on his face and suffocated him with her twat and laughed and laughed and giggled and was silly like I'd never seen her. I never actually knew at that time what twat meant which makes me think she was very mature for her age which was only seven though it could be that I was somewhat backward.

The day Mr. Farley died Parnell came to school and I yelled "What's the matter fart-breath?" and he hated me with his look and said "My Dad's dead." When I got home Yvonne and Bob from next door were there. Everyone's face was black with the mouths turned down. I said "Mr. Farley's dead." "Eat your lunch Ida," was all. "How did he die?" I asked. "He gassed himself down at the gravel pit." It seemed alright to me but everyone looked down at their coffee and the room stank with their fear so I ate my lunch and went down to the gully to sort the thing out. Old Farley drank like a fish and beat up on his family. Nobody liked him. He didn't seem to hold all that much affection for himself either. He was not in tune so to speak with any thing or any body. I'd even thought of killing him once after he kicked my spokes in. So Farley's dead. So what? People have no sense. I got back to school just as Miss Bird rang the bell and couldn't help spending the afternoon wondering at the mechanics of gassing.

A gravel pit, when you think of it, is an appropriate site for suicide. Farley's choice was purely practical: nobody would come by to interrupt. But Ida never lost the thought that perhaps he was more than he seemed.

When I was young someone somewhere took me fishing. The only reason, so far as I can tell, was that he loved both fishing and me; though I confess, at this late date, that I may be making mountains out of fishing trips so to speak. My old Dad loved me and never asked for anything back. So sings memory.

I'm lying: he asked for everything back. He wouldn't speak of it but when I knew I did what I could.

Ida thought maybe he was bent or something. It seemed a queer request that she just keep talking all the time: she'd been at it for two hours now and felt a little silly. He even looked a bit fruity with that clear smooth skin and those skinny little wrists. Probably just spaced out on too much dope or something. Nearly everybody was these days. Even the farm boys were popping the odd pill. Licker's still quicker, she mused and felt like giggling but his poker face stopped her. Maybe his mother died, she thought.

It didn't take me as long as some to find out what a waterass Jesus actually was though Lucy helped. I happened to mention how funny it seemed that all the losers around just had to act like losers and they got a brownie badge or something for being so great. Well, she looked up at me like a real friend. It wasn't always like that, she said. Once upon a time it was the truly happy strong people who were number one. People with backbone who knew how to laugh and have a good time without worrying about it. But as usual there were more creeps around than anything and they got together and made the whole thing up about Jesus etcetera just to get us sucked in so they wouldn't stand out as such sickly types and could get us all down and win in the end. *They* got to be number one. Blessed are the meek, weak and creepy, right?

Luke thought, I can't move, jesus god I can't move a muscle or I'll lose my mind. If I smile goddamn I lose my mind. His thoughts raced through a confusion of memory and fantasy without regard for order, with no sense of control; they breathed light and shadow onto all that had gone before and all that had yet to come but all he could think was: I'll lose my mind. If I blow it I'm dead. Hold on just for a while. Just a little while.

My brother used to trap weasel and muskrat in the winters and sell the pelts to the Hudson's Bay. You might think I'm making this up the world being so modern and whatnot but it's a fact. By way of his trapping he came to know old Indian Joe well enough to get him to make some moccasins for him so I even met him once myself though when he brought them over my Mom wouldn't let him in the house and it was freezing cold as well. I hung around while Chuck paid him and was absolutely tongue-tied. He was so much like a real Indian: he wore an old hat with a feather and had a greasy braid and everything. One time after that I was sitting in a snowdrift on the other side of the gully scared to go home I was so wet when Indian Joe came walking and I yelled "Hey!" but he didn't look up even so I yelled "Hey You! It's me, Ida Johnson!" so he had to look up then. But he just shuddered and looked in me black and crazy and walked on without saying hello or anything.

Even as a small child Lucy understood the inherent limitations of her own circumstance. She was female, poor, and Indian in a male, material, white world. Her life seemed a predetermined one that left little room for manoeuvre. If she could adopt enough dull reason, if she could stand that white stain, she might scrape through the tenth grade. Then the government would condescend to send her off for a two year course from which she might emerge a full-fledged bonafide nurses' aide. If she refused the offer but was able to arouse a sense of enterprise and initiative in herself she might sell cunt in Calgary; more than likely she would stay on the Reserve and the cunt would be free for the taking. According to precedent she'd grow fat and tired and take to whiskey in an imitative attempt to deaden the nerves, to protect herself from the weight of responsibility. The course of her likely dissipation might seem typically Indian but the real longed-for effect: surrender of will: is a universal compulsion.

She never did sort out the logisitics of avoiding the inevitable; for one thing she knew that the fantasy which is planning is worse than sitting thick and dull where you are; but avoid she did.

Different though Lucy and Ida seemed there had been a meeting of mind and spirit there: long ago in the gully, two young girls playing into twilight, loving one another without knowing. Ida was seldom over- whelmed by Lucy's fierce energy and interminable pronouncements. "Coyotes lie," she might say. "If you believe in lies you're dead." "Jeez," Ida would counter, "you got to lie to stay out of trouble sometimes." The stolid reasonableness of her responses exasperated Lucy and seemed further proof of her friend's half- wittedness.

Still, there was something about Ida that caught her off guard: a certain gleam behind the eye, a sureness sometimes in her touch. It was as though she feigned stupidity. But for what reason?

Lucy would miss Ida but she couldn't stay in Longview. She couldn't breathe. Too many people took her time and filled it with waste. She was bored crazy at the school with its emphasis on sequence and structure, on the memorization of what was tried and, she knew, patently untrue. But what oppressed her past endurance was the town's lack of humour. The whites were tight with misery.

The air was clear back home. It seemed a good place to move and grow. But the illusion of unlimited space was shortlived. In time she recognized that the ease of her own people was itself a pose. They lacked hardness. They were as frightened of light as the rest and again, she couldn't stay.

Lucy left the Reserve for Port Moody, Basel, Athabasca, Coeur-de-laine, Sault Ste. Marie, London, Wenatchee, Port au Prince, Scotsguard, Kamloops, Ramnes, Röcken, Thunder Bay, Fort St. John, Hollywood, Prague, Milo, Lloydminster, Munich...

She worked as a deckhand, a mothers' help, a dancer, a cook, a trucker, a hooker, a cashier, a movie star, a cowboy, a clown...

In the end the outrageous energy wasn't enough: she needed somebody with a will to match her own so she came back looking for Ida.

I was going to be thirteen and my mother kept at me to have a party but I said no. *N O* as I was too old to have a stupid birthday party. Naturally enough I got a cake for it though and a transistor which I'd wanted for years and a brassiere from my godmother at which my mother went pftt and I hated her she was so dumb and such an embarrassment. I met Derek in the gully and he gave me some smokes and the two of us lit up and fooled around and I showed him my bra and he undid his fly and took a pee and didn't put it back in and was waving it around and said, what do you think this is? It was stiff as a broom and I said it was alright and he said what do you call it? and I said dink and he said no, it was a cock and came up and kissed me and the cock poked into my stomach and all the while he was pushing down my pedal pushers with the elasticized waist and I felt funny like a soft furry watermelon was pushing down between my legs and he put his fingers inside me it was sopping wet and the cock was bobbing around and poking my stomach and Derek said please and looked funny so I said sure and he said touch it so I did and he laid me down and got the cock just there between my legs and yelped and twitched and I was really a sticky mess and smelled of bleach and I thought hell's bells so I said "I love you Derek" and he, "I love you Ida."

When Ida turned thirteen she got a transistor radio, some writing paper, nylons, an emerald green blouse, a bra (28AA), and a birthday-wrapped box of cotton wool with nothing inside. No one knew about this last gift; she found it in the gully behind the house. There was no mistaking who it was for. The card read: "To Ida," signed, "A friend in need is a friend indeed." There was, in addition, a rather cryptic message scrawled beneath the address.

> *Everyone decides once. A very few choose to choose.*
> *The rest choose not to.*

But Ida couldn't make head nor tail of that. She dismissed it as nonsense and turned instead to the stuff that was nothing. (Ida was always what you might call a careless reader.) Without regard for meaning or consequence she proceeded to eat what she could of the cotton wool itself. When she had done she crammed the bland remains into every orifice she could find on her young body.

On the way home she stopped at the Chinaman's and bought a pack of Players. Her Dad said, "No. There'll be no smoking in this house," and she said, "Fine. I'll sit on the goddamned step."

She never discovered the source of the gift though she heard later that someone strange had been seen hanging around the hotel that day. He looked foreign, they said, but couldn't say for sure. He spoke to no one. He was small-built and wore riding boots and sunglasses according to Mrs. 'Gawk' Gregory at the Post Office.

Ida got married because she had to. No one was surprised. Statistics indicate that the last time a local girl got married for reasons less well defined was in 1948 and she (Rosalind Clark was her name) was explained away after losing her marbles in '49. There is absolutely no logic in that explanation but who argues with fact?

I was at your wedding but you wouldn't have noticed me in that cast of thousands. In Longview they do it up right. You even made a special trip to Calgary for the dress and it was some dress Ida—lace on silk on satin over your swelling belly. You didn't miss a thing: something old (you, Ida?), something new (the baby there), something borrowed (the whole razmatazzled show), something blue ('something' that made your smile stay red and solid like frozen meat). I got pretty drunk in the end myself and started talking to a few of the riggers who'd come in for the celebration. I expressed some amazement at your age when one of them laughed surprise that you weren't caught up long ago. "But she's only fourteen," I said. "Fuck man, most of them are bleeding like stuck pigs before they're ten around here."

We didn't get home from the hall till real late. What with my feet being so sore with the shoes and with everyone expecting traditionally for us to get off home *early* I kept at him from midnight on but he was real drunk so I had no luck. When we did get home the trailer was so overfull with all the presents and whatnot we could hardly get in the door. I just got the light on and he grabbed my neck and said suck me off so I did with my going-away suit on and everything but he couldn't come and my jaw hurt so I had to cry some but he just shoved it in further and finally he came though with somewhat of a whimper if I do say so myself.

When we got married it was fairly dull. I was fairly lonely there as Derek didn't like hanging around with just me so he'd go off somewheres and I'd watch the TV and eat. Actually I got pretty fat then. In the beginning I'd just tell myself it's the baby but of course I knew and Derek would say pig at me and I'd try to diet say on tomatoes and coffee then just eat about six loaves of bread and jam like crazy I'd get so funny about it. Of course after Deb was born I had lots to do and then I lost most of that ugly fat as they say though I did get on to smoking an awful lot. Well. I wasn't going to have any more kids after that first and told Derek so. He was glad actually and I got on the pill and everything I wasn't going to be tied down forever but then I thought well Jesus why the hell not, what's the bloody difference, so I just stopped taking it without telling Derek and said the pill couldn't have worked so it seemed then to be nobody's fault. He got all set to sue Bailey the druggist and everything as Derek's the kind of guy who'd kill anybody he figured had done him a wrong sometime or other but I talked him out of it, lucky for me eh? And I liked Danny better than Deb, like he was my idea or something.

Derek Campbell's subjugation of Ida was not deliberately harmful. He thought he loved her and the rest followed. At any rate the particulars of LOVE circa Longview 1960 indicate so.

You couldn't actually say I liked Derek in the sense for instance of his creepy personality but I loved him; we were truly in love. He wasn't an outgoing person at all if you understand me, he didn't like people much. I mean he liked his friends you know but anybody else made him nervous, made him feel a loser, so he'd get real mad and hate them for making him feel rotten and that's why he got into so many fights and stuff is what I think now. But he was good. Lots didn't care for him, but he was a good provider and we always had plenty money and he didn't drink all the time like some I know. At first when we were going around together I didn't like the fact of his not allowing me to talk with other boys or the way he'd get so terrible mad about me wearing too much stuff on my face or my skirts too short. It was like he wanted me to be a fucking nun or something though he sure as hell made me do a few things that even a fucking nun wouldn't be caught dead at. Ha! There's my Baptist churching showing eh? But I got used to it. I got used to being a quiet sort of person till I couldn't remember not being so.

Sure he slept with other girls but only when he had to, like near the end of the two times I was expecting, so I couldn't say much could I? I admit I'd get into awful depressed moods over it but Derek would get so mad I'd have to quit it and be happy.

I'll tell you that nothing seems very clear to me, not even myself, though I'm sure I was once very strong and clear-sighted if I remember correctly. There never seemed to be much choice in the matter so how could I be blamed for any of it I ask you? Besides, and I've wondered about this, it doesn't seem as though anything I've expected to happen with regards to strong feelings from myself has happened. For instance, I know I never loved one person as I once thought loving somebody should be. Now I'll bet you're thinking I'm a terrible person but none of it's deliberate so how can I be? I think sometimes what's the stupid point but even there it never goes beyond as I can't get worked up about anything, not even the births of my kids which I've heard others say to be a really great thing but what I took to be more a giant pain in the cunt (excuse my parlez-vous). If there really aren't such things as you're led to believe such as love or even real hate or just happiness then you should see it clear and not be made to lie at it so you fool even yourself maybe. Lucy used to tell me I could do anything I wanted if I decided and at that time I believed her as it seemed a very clear-cut thing but as time went on I seemed to get rather clouded and things happened that I never decided about once.

Imagery left to cramp inside the mind self-destructs.
It explodes or, more probably, expires.

Lack of air. Lack of *Lebensraum*?

On the morning of October 15, 1965 Ida took Debbie and the baby over to her Mom's house where she did a wash and drank four cups of coffee. She brought the kids home for lunch: she and Deb had Kraft dinner and Cokes; Danny had Gerber carrots and a bottle. After putting them to bed she watched *As The World Turns* on TV and asked Carole over for coffee. Carole gave her an oven mitt as a birthday gift and stayed with the kids while Ida collected her dried laundry. It was a cold clear bright day with a high of 36°F. Derek came home for supper at five and they had sirloin steaks for supper. Ida and Debbie ate butterscotch pudding for dessert. Derek declined the pudding, drank a quart of milk straight from the carton, told Ida she was getting fat again then left to play hockey (defense) in High River. Ida ironed until nine and let the kids stay up with her for company. After putting them to bed she watched part of a variety show from Calgary and at last the movie which she thinks was funny but can't remember for sure. Derek came home just as it ended. He'd been drinking but not much; they had coffee and he told her about the game. He gave her a Borg jacket for her birthday. She exclaimed over it for him then had one panic-stricken moment when she thought she'd run out of cigarettes but Derek saved the day by bringing in a whole carton from the car. They each had another smoke before getting into bed. Ida thought Derek seemed depressed and suggested they make love to thank him properly for the jacket. They did: Ida on top. It took a long time but it was alright. Derek kissed her and said she wasn't really getting fat. She had another cigarette. Derek fell asleep. Ida can't remember if she slept in the meantime or not but at four she thought she heard someone outside. She put

Derek's coat on and opened the door. There was no one there but she sensed otherwise and went right out into the dark. There was a terrific blast and the trailer was a ball of flame. Somebody said "Don't cry Ida" but she didn't understand because she wasn't crying.

*

The morning wore on and a variety of regulars filtered in for coffee and doughnuts, coffee and pie, or just plain coffee. Shirl seemed to be on intimate terms with everyone and kept up a steady patter of mindless anecdote. Luke watched with wonder and forgot why he was there. She complained non-stop to each and every customer about dishpan hands, her kids' ringworm, the lousy weather, rising prices, her old man's bullying, and imminent world-wide catastrophe. But she glowed with affirmation and energy and filled the room with warmth.

"It's nice here," Luke said in a sudden expanse of feeling.

"Are you kidding?"

"No. It's nice. She's nice. You're nice." He took Ida's hand and kissed the palm. "You're nice," he repeated.

That's downright sentimental, she wanted to say. But her heart was pounding in her ears. "You're funny," she said. "But I like you."

"Go on," he said. "It's a good story. You tell a good story."

I couldn't get to sleep. I kept thinking dear Ida dear Ida dear Ida like an old crazy stuck record. And the wind goddamned wind Alberta wind blowing cans around the incinerator and a door somewhere banging like a song. There was no moon. I went outside thinking I heard someone call. Well, I don't know what with that wind. Still, somebody calling me. Ida. Ida. Like a whisper so it's stupid to think. In all that wind who could hear a whisper? I thought it was Lucy. The black scared me and the wind and the sounds I couldn't see. Then suddenly everything still and clear, fear lifting like a fog. I went inside for the bread knife and put it back for the meat cleaver. I killed him first. Quick. Not a sound. A clean clean perfect clean slice down through the throat past the throat through the neck not quite through. Clean. And his blood so red and thick I didn't know. I kissed him. Blood thick in my mouth and my nose, in my hair. Thick and red and good. The babies. Clean quick slice slice like a butcher. I'm a butcher. Everything red and clear as a bell. I turned the gas on. I had a shower and set my hair. I did a manicure under the dryer. Clean nightgown white and crisp and cool. Derek's coat, matches and a pack of Players in the pocket. Outside. I lit a smoke and threw it in through the door. The sky was red and clear as a bell.

What did you do after the fire?

You mean right after?

Well, you know...

I went to Calgary. It was fantastic. I really did. I went to Calgary. Got a ride with the waterman's wife who was going in for something or other. I really did. And it was fantastic.

What do you mean? You'd been before.

Yeah sure but not like that. There was always a reason before. Not like that. Anything could happen that's how I felt. Anything. And hell I wasn't scared or anything I just thought I'm going to Calgary and anything can happen. I sang Carter family stuff all the way in and drove Mrs. Kitt nuts with it.

So what happened?

Oh Jesus it was fantastic. I got a job. It's easy to get a job if you're not particular like some. I got a job waiting tables in the Holiday Inn. Really posh and the Americans, you know, the Americans tip like crazy, I had piles of money and the hotel rented rooms cheap for staff if you wanted. But the thing was how I felt. It's a terrible thing losing your family like that then feeling so good right after but I don't know I'm just telling you there's no point lying about it. Is there? I never did one thing that I, myself, didn't decide. For months and months I just did what I wanted. Yeah I still remember that. I still remember how fantastic it was.

Why did it end?

I don't know. It just passed and I had to go home. I don't know why that either but I had to go home in the end.

*

This guy came into the Inn and I just thought Oh god I got to have that. When I brought him the denver sandwich I said "My name's Ida how'd you like to come home with me?" Just like that I said it and I'd never done such a thing or even thought about it in my whole life but it seemed to be the right thing to do never mind all the bullshit. Well he went beet red and I felt a little sorry for that but by god he was cool as anything in a minute and said "That's fine Ida, I'd like that fine" and smiled and his name was Wayne and he was as good as I knew.

From then on in it was the best year of my life. I was making guys all the time without a thought just as they struck my fancy so to speak. I was closer to acting like me than I've ever been in company. No bullshit. I got together with this Wayne every once in awhile for a few laughs but nothing serious happened. We just got on good and liked each other. It's my opinion nothing serious ever happens if you keep clear of the bullshit. As time went by however I couldn't keep it up and got more and more into dreaming and mooning about romance and crap like that. I started to not like being alone and thought about things I shouldn't have. I had to go home. I was coming down and I had to go home to see my Dad.

Lucy's incessant wandering, her inability to locate either a time or a place that seemed specifically hers led her to believe that this time around was maybe her last. Sometimes, she was so convinced of her own supra-human qualities that she felt her coming at all (October 15, 1950) was a terrible mistake. But on whose part? she couldn't help but wonder. And that question would drive her down again.

In the spring of '66 Lucy got a small part in an obscure American film and spent three weeks on location near Port-au-Prince. She played the Haitian mistress of a Belgian arms dealer mysteriously involved in a voodoo plot to overthrow the U.S. government. Her big scene took place at a ceremonial ritual during which she succumbs to the spirit of Uncle Samedi and tears a live chicken apart (breast from wing so to speak). What terrified her was the extent to which she merged souls with that ridiculous one-dimensional character she portrayed.

Everything was so well organized. Somebody said "Start screaming," and she did. The blacks shuddered, their yellow eyes turned to slits and that goddamn chicken she'd never catch the chicken. There was a throb somewhere. Drums! Yes drums for Chrissake. It's a movie. It's a movie. It's only a movie. But that high-pitched wail was bugging her. It's me, she thought. It's me. Still it went on and on, nothing to do with her, the sweat pouring, somebody thrusting the chicken at her. It squawked and clawed to match her screams and wouldn't be still; all she could see were yellow slits and the arms dealer. She bit hard into the neck of the bird for ballast and tore a great piece of flesh bone and feather away with her. The bird squawked on but the screams stopped as she buried her face in the hole she had made.

Somebody yelled "PRINT!"

I'd just never forget that year in Calgary. I was only eighteen but I owned the world, every bit of it—was how I felt. Everything that happened, it was me who made it happen. There wasn't anything I didn't decide on. Margaret, the head girl in the dining room there once told me to quit 'strutting' all over the place. That's what she said mind you. Strutting! Wayne said I was the only woman he'd ever known that didn't weigh a man down. I didn't want him down. I decided that. I was Ace in the hole. I didn't want anybody down though there were lots who were. Me too in the end. I don't know. It just started slipping away into thin air. My strength like. Something, anyway. I could feel it slip.

What I really wanted bad was to be a singer in a band. At one time I had about three hundred of those Hit Parade song magazines and so help me I bet I knew every song in them. It's not that my voice was all that good or anything but I sure had all the expressions and movements down pat since I practised with a mirror nearly every day and my brother had stacks of records that I got a lot of the tunes from not to mention the radio, but after I got to be older I didn't actually care anymore in that the whole idea seemed farfetched and stupid. Anyway, what's funny is that when I came home again after that year in Calgary I got to telling Dave Shields about it at the Chinaman's where I went for a coke and the jukebox mostly. Dave said he knew a guy in Black Diamond who was getting a group together and that he'd drive me up there sometime, so I said when and he said tonight so I said yeah okay but my Mom was real mad at such a thing for some reason or other. I said "Hell, I can't just mope around all my life for Chrissake" and put on my new blue stretch pants. Dave came at seven in his new Merc which was neat by the way and off we rode, me very excited and happy. We got up there and Dave said "Do you want to go in for a beer?" and me that I probably couldn't get in, I had no ID, so he said "I'll pick up a couple of boxes then" and actually came out with four. At this house we went to I met Roger who was going to start a band and we all had four or five beers then he asked "Are you going to do your stuff or what?" and I said "Sure," not nervous anymore because of the beer though still excited and everything, so I stood by the dinette table and sang *It Wasn't God Who Made Honky Tonk Angels* like a real pro if you ask me. Roger said "I don't know honey, can you sex it up a little?" so I sang *Jambalaya* next and he said "Better," and "Come here." He said I was the best he'd heard so far and he'd let me know as soon as he got things straightened out and he put his arms around me really gentle and kissed me such as Derek used to years ago so I let him touch me where he wanted to, I mean I was no lily of the valley myself or anything, and I started to stroke his cock through the jeans which was hard but Dave got up then and said don't leave me out. Whereas I wasn't in favour of him coming in on it, Roger said that Dave was a good buddy so what the hell. We drank some more beer and I played records, Roger having millions, and over that time we all got our clothes off and were fooling around in general both of them slurping around my crack like it was cream cheese and I got pretty horny myself in the beginning but the two of them looked so dumb I lost that and though they both stuck it to me in the end, if you ask me all along they were much the more interested in taking swipes at each other's balls.

*

You said you went home after Calgary?

Yeah. To my parents.

For how long?

A week or so. I guess I stayed a week.

Then?

What? Well, I went up to the Diamond in case Roger had to get in touch with me. I got a job and a room at the Black Diamond Hotel.

Did he get in touch?

No. Dave told me he'd gone up to work in Leduc.

Did you think to go up after him?

I may be slow boy but I'm not entirely lacking.

Pardon?

I may be slow but I ain't dumb.

I stayed on in the Diamond nearly a year. My old friend Faye was living there and my brother and his family had a new house just over in Turner Valley so I wasn't stuck for company or anything. My Dad came up once. He came into the coffee shop and said "Do you think you'd like to go on a fishing trip Ida?" and I said "Sure, why not" and nearly started to cry for some reason. I went and quit the job and pretty soon we were barrelling right along up the Highwood in the old Chevy. My Dad said there were some good holes up Kananaskis way and I was real happy: I'd never been so far up as that though as it turned out we never got so high after all. We turned off at Deadman's Creek where we knew of a beaver dam. I caught two Rainbow right off but one I had to throw back and my Dad I think got five or six so we had a good feed. I made us some coffee. It was a fantastic night, cold as anything but jesus with my Dad and the fire and good coffee and good smokes...It was fantastic. "Did you kill them?" my old Dad asked. "Yeah." "I thought that," he said but never said anything more. We stayed up for two weeks and never left the fishing being so good. One day he said "I got to be back at the plant tomorrow." "I know," I said. I didn't but I'd supposed it would come. "What are you going to do?" he asked. "I don't know" and I didn't either. "The MacPhersons need help in their cookhouse," he told me.

Ida droned on in a flat monotone. It was nearly noon. Her eyes were flat with fatigue and boredom. Easier to lay on your back, she thought. Luke watched her lack of interest with amazement. In all his life he'd never known anyone to tire talking about themselves. She hadn't even begun with enthusiasm. But he sat captivated and sought for clues in every phrase. What gave her such resilience? He'd been with her so long—watched her rise and fall and, always, rise again. Now she was fallen: spiritless, with no trace of regeneration to come. But rise she would. He wanted to know why.

Yeah. I went to the MacPhersons' alright. Stayed a bloody year too. The old lady was a regular slave-driver if you ask me. Are you asking me? Hey. That was a joke. Boy, have you got a lousy sense of humour!

The MacPhersons' specialization was people; cows were an incidental concern. The place didn't look like a dude ranch: that was precisely the reason so many paid so much for the privilege of staying a week or a month with that colourless Scots family high in the Alberta foothills. Two hundred dollars a week gave you a bed in a bunkhouse and three starchy meals a day; five hundred a shingled bit of shack in the midst of the spruce that backed up the mountain behind the main buildings. There was no heated pool, no bar and discotheque, not even running water. Service was not included. The retreat was so popular that bookings were made three and four years in advance. Year after year they came, earnestly masquerading as plain simple folk, denying their wealth, embarrassed by it (momentarily), and all the while flaunting the same with that new fully outfitted jeep they'd picked up in Calgary especially for the trip or the carefully soiled and unco-ordinated clothes they wore with self-conscious abandon. For some the crude surroundings were a re-creation of their past, metaphorically anyway; for the rest it was a more honest attempt to make fantasy fact. They had the money to try. It was like going to summer camp or living a movie; some even supposed it was like being young again. This is the life, they thought, this is the life. In the end they were bored silly and made furtive notes to themselves to find an analyst back in Phoenix or Toronto or Minneapolis to discover what was wrong that they couldn't live like 'real' people.

Ida got a hundred dollars a month plus room and board for helping Mrs. MacPherson in the cookhouse. In effect this meant hauling, peeling, and boiling potatoes though she also cooked great tubs of porridge in the morning and was responsible for all the dish-washing that had to be done. There were never less than twelve at the table including Mr. Mac who was right out of it, the old lady and her boys (Aleister, Will, and John Jr.: all in their late forties) and Lars the hired man. Ida got up at five-thirty to light the stove, set the table, and start the porridge, had an hour to herself in the morning and another midafternoon, and was usu-ally finished everything by eight-thirty or nine at night.

*

I never really mixed with the guests as I figured we wouldn't have much in common and be stuck for topics of conversation for instance. At first I kept pretty well to myself but of course in time it's funny how you get to know other people just by being around them not even talking or anything until one day you're comfortable with one or two then another so you get to mix that way. Lars was my favourite though I admit not in the beginning. He was an old Swede, and I mean old, who'd been with the Macs for years and years. When he got drunk which was fairly often he'd call me Hjordes and weep just sit in his chair and cry to himself real quiet like but I knew. My best time was in the mornings early before anybody else was around even in the winter when it was pitch black. I liked being the one who fired the stove. Even when it was freezing I liked the smell and the feel of being the one who got it all going. The cats would all come hang around meowing and carrying on for their milk and the warm and I liked that too. It seemed as long as I was alone anywhere everything moved right and was as it should be somehow but then when people got into the picture it all cluttered up and I wasn't myself.

In all these years you know I've never met one person I could just sit with and be like I am by myself.

What about Lucy?

Well, no. In spite of her being my best friend she made me feel sort of dumb all the time. Like I was a disappointment to her or something.

76

I got pretty sick of all the goddamn work I was doing and of Mrs. Mac's whining and complaining but looking back now it was fairly good like I needed that year just to have a little time. I thought Jesus H, I can't stay up here in the sticks all my life I got to get out in the world, that was my attitude but after a whole year I'd only saved eight hundred dollars as you have to buy smokes and O Henrys and beer and stuff to survive, and knowing like I do the price of butter I knew it was fuckall so I thought, I'll get them, and I did. Now I've never been awfully bright but there are a few things I know about, one being that old farts wasting time and money out at some dump like that are really screwed around and another being that you don't have to do much to screw somebody who's already screwed around if you get my meaning. Anyway. I made six thousand bucks in two months being 'a real person' to twelve of those limp-pricked ranch guests. The reason I say that is just that seven of them actually called me that. A real person, I mean. "Ida," they said, "*you* are a real person." Hell, who isn't you know but I wasn't going to say nothing.

Ida went about her work like a real pro. They were always eyeing her anyway, not that she was especially good to look at; it was more a case of being the only piece of stray meat around. If she'd merely set out to exploit their sexual fantasies the most she could have hoped to gain was twenty maybe twenty-five bucks a head. Instead she titillated their hunger for myth, the whole reason they were there in the first place. Rather than ignore them with a glaze over her eyes and the muscles in her face slack and sullen, she would meet their gaze full on then quickly drop her eyes and blush or burn her finger as though it were a mistake —she hadn't meant to be so brazen. So they warmed to her from the beginning, feeling special, and smiled. She would single one out from a particular group and slowly, carefully, focus all of her artful little attentions on him. In line with the setting he would forgive her bad odours and ragged complexion, regard her inarticulateness as innocence and her imperfections as natural beauty. After two or three days of meaningful glances, nervous smiles and extra spoonfuls of potato she would contrive an accidental meeting away from the others and somehow stammer "Hello" or "Excuse me," look like a scared rabbit and make as if to run. "Wait," he would invariably say. "What's your name?" "Ida," she'd whisper. From there it was easy. Sometimes she'd fuck the man and sometimes not. What mattered was to always always follow him with adoring, suffocating eyes. She hardly ever spoke. By the end of his stay not only did the whole lifestyle bore him to death but Ida too; yet he thought it must be his fault and in the end would hand her a plain white envelope to assuage his guilt. "You know honey it just wouldn't work out." Ida would sit mute and let her muscles sag. It was over.

One day after that I said to the old lady "Well, I'll be leaving then" and of course everyone was real surprised thinking I had no get up and go and probably that I'd still be there in a hundred years. One of the boys went down to Longview once a week to load up on food and whatnot so I got a ride. Aleister let me off in front of the hotel and gave me ten bucks as we were shaking hands goodbye. I had to laugh at that with the six nearly seven thousand in my purse. I didn't even go home or look anybody up I just waited outside the hotel there for the bus into Calgary. My plan was to hit out and see a bit of the world so to speak and I thought maybe I'd go to Banff first which I'd heard of but never actually been to. It was five and dark by the time we pulled into Calgary and as per usual I was starved so I went into the cafe there at the depot to get some food and got to talking with these two guys who were hippies, the first I'd ever seen actually, and you know they were really friendly. They'd been hitching around the whole country for months but said it was getting too cold so they were going to bus it to Vancouver which was like the tropics or something. "Why don't you come?" they asked. "Okay." "Farout," said the one called Billy.

Once on that bus we just yakked on and on for hours telling stories true and false etcetera. It was real nice, everything so quiet and the dark outside but the little yellow lights just above your seat making spots of warm right where you sat eating O Henrys smoking up a storm. I was glad I'd decided to go although I did have my doubts for a minute when the one called Ken told me I was a real person. Just as I was falling off to sleep someone began to stroke my head and whispered "You'll like the coast Ida, no snow." Well, hell I like snow but I didn't say anything as it didn't seem important.

When I woke up I thought: I'm dead and gone to hell. I'll tell you now that I hate mountains. We were right in the middle of them and though it was daylight everything was dark and gloomy and full of giant shadows. I hold the opinion that mountains are stupid, they look stupid, but at that time I was too afraid of falling over a cliff to figure out what exactly I thought about them. Billy asked if I was going to puke I looked so pale but I said no and we got talking again and stopped at Cache Creek for eats and before you know it we're out of the mountains and soon after dark again we're in Vancouver. When I got off the bus I thought, if only Lucy could see me now! which was funny as I hadn't thought of her for ages.

When we got outside the depot it was raining cats and dogs. I thought we should wait for it to let up but Billy told me we'd probably wait till April so we walked in the wet awhile and tried to hitch a ride but had no luck so gave up and caught a city bus. Billy said, "You got a sleeping bag?" Well I didn't know we were going to camp out somewhere so I said "What for?" and he, "To sleep in. The house has lots of floor space but that's about it." I guess I gave him a stunned look because he said "Never mind, we'll share mine." And that, if I do say so myself, was the most low-keyed proposition I'd ever had in my life.

I tell you I was as excited as ever I'd been. I didn't know anybody but Billy and Ken and there wasn't a soul in the whole city that knew me. I felt like yelling "HEY! LOOK AT ME!!" a hundred times and I kept jumping around and everything. I actually did yell once but Ken and Billy just grinned at me instead of being pissed off.

Ida never forgave Ken his thoughtless remark; she denied him her favours and he, accordingly, disappeared from view. But she liked Billy and stayed with him over the winter. He wrote poetry and played the guitar—both badly—and wanted to homestead somewhere north of Fort St. John. Ida had been around long enough to know that this pale undernourished frightened boy from Don Mills Ont. was as likely to take up homesteading as she was the cello but she didn't want to dirt farm anyway so that didn't matter.

It was a bad winter. Everything conspired to deplete her waning energies once and for all: the rain, the gloomy house, the spiritless lethargy of its inhabitants, the rain. And she lost her money. Ida never particularly trusted anyone but Billy was so passive and unthreatening that when he asked how it was she could afford to feed and clothe them she told him. She never confused passive with unthreatening again.

Billy had a plan. Day after day he lay curled in his sleeping bag or sat mute by the fire while his slow childish brain churned out reel after reel of his own success movie. I'll show them all, he thought. I'm somebody! If a guy could make the right connection you could pick up to sixty kilos of dope for $6000. Jesus. At ten bucks an ounce cheap that's say 2.2x60= 132x16=2112x10=21,120. Fucking Jesus! $21,120. That's $15,000 clear profit! Jesus, oh jesus.

He met up with an American dealer called Pisces who agreed to fly $5000 worth of dope up from Oregon for $1000. Billy would have to arrange for the stuff to be transported from the Abbotsford airstrip himself. He was almost hysterical with panic: where would he stash that much dope? what chances did a plane have to land unseen out there? where could he get a truck? Jesus: but the fantasy had him by the balls. They shook hands and Billy handed over Ida's money.

He didn't tell Ida. He wanted to wait until it was over, until he had the profits, or at least the goods, in hand. But a week went by and no phone call came. When she discovered the money gone he went carefully over the whole enterprise with such enthusiasm that she said nothing. A month later she packed a shopping bag and her old blue suitcase. "Billy," she said. "You're a tit."

*

She was back where she started: where she had started half a dozen times before. Broke. No job. Nowhere particular to go. She hadn't made any friends. The people she'd met through Billy were soft. They had no colour. She distrusted them now. Like you'd distrust a jew, she thought and wondered why she thought about jews so much. She'd never known any for Chrissake.

Once again as luck would have it I got a job right off cleaning tables in a cafeteria at some University. At first, by the looks of things, namely all the young people, I thought maybe I'd get to meet a lot of people and strike up new acquaintances but students and such don't seem to care to mix with people of my station in life or so I noticed. I thought then maybe I should take advantage of my situation and take up learning but it fell through as it seemed books had nothing to do with me so I bought a transistor. I'm lying, actually I took it from a coat.

I found this little house for forty a month in some lady's backyard and moved in right away. I really believe it had once been a play house it was so tiny. It had a flush toilet in a cupboard by itself then a single brown iron bed and some drawers a fridge hotplate and sink one straight chair and one easy. I could hardly turn around and could just stand up me only 5'2" (eyes of blue Ha!) so you can imagine. But I loved it as it was private and my own. I was very excited. I bought a tablecloth and actually made *by hand* my own curtains from some sunny-coloured yellow cotton after getting my first pay. I used to come home there after work and fry up a bunch of bacon and bread and eat and take off my clothes and just be there enjoying myself but soon of course it seemed too much and I'd have to just sleep all the time or go crazy with myself filling up the room till I couldn't breathe. I wrote my Dad a letter.

> *Dear Dad,*
>
> *Hi how are you? I'm fine as far as it goes. I got a job at Simon Fraser University how about that!!? It rains all the time here. I got lots of friends and am real popular. What would you say to me making a visit home? I was just wondering. Well I've got to be going now. Bye for now.*
>
> > *Sincerely,*
> > *your daughter,*
> > *Ida*
>
> *ps Say hello to Mom for me*

I never actually got a reply back. I believe I must have neglected to give them my address or something.

Did you ever have your very own face come at you out of nowhere? I did once, back there in Vancouver. It followed me around for three days. It was the face I'd always had and I knew then I'd have it forever like a judgement. It was everywhere and made me look at it. I expect everyone's surprised at the things that take place such as growing old or finding yourself living with a certain person or even in regard to things you say. I've got this idea that everybody's exactly the same from beginning to end no matter what happens large or small. At any rate I'm that way myself. I feel today exactly like I ever did. My face was so lonely and peculiar I never got over it.

Lucy, meanwhile, sits resolutely alone in a Munich beerhall. It's her night off from the Krazy Lady cabaret where she has top billing as Gregor the Georgian juggler. The Germans think she's a queer little fellow. They humour her but she has no friends. "There goes Gregor," they laugh. "He's so fast with his balls the ladies can't get at them."

The Germans are pigs, she thinks. She has come to the beerhall to get drunk, to find a friend, to lose her sight. And all she can think is 'the Germans are pigs'. She is running down, she can feel it. And she's running out of possibilities that appeal.

Where do you go when it's time to go home and you have none? Sitting there, trapped behind the noise and confusion she sees the full implications of her peculiar quest and is filled with dread. She thinks immediately of Ida as she often does in moments of despair but is as yet unable to register the fact that she is also thinking of her salvation. Nevertheless, she manages to get a message through:

> I am frozen in loneliness.
> Only fools and goats climb so high.

I was working the evening shift cleaning up trays and whatnot. Hardly anyone was there as we were soon closing down but this one guy real goodlooking and obviously some big shot maybe even a professor type was sitting staring at me and I thought 'Jesus' as it was somewhat creepy. Eventually I had to wipe his table of course and he said "It's a strange night" which I thought was a pretty dumb thing for openers but I said "Yeah" just to say something. He was rolling a Players which I thought to be pretty cool. He said "You're very beautiful." Now I know I'm not *that* but it was nice anyway. "You're vintage Fifties. Did you ever have a boyfriend with a fifty-four Ford?" I didn't know what he was on about so I just said "Yeah" again. "I'd like to fuck you," he said. Well hell I had to give him points for being so direct. And it could be interesting. "Okay," I said. "I'm done here in about ten minutes." His mouth smiled but his eyes were dead. "Sometime," he said, "sometime we will" and took off like a bat out of hell. I think he hated me. You meet all sorts.

Ida dropped a tray. The noise nudged the professor out of his reverie just long enough to catch a glimpse of her bent and awkward over the broken cups and soggy cigarette ends. A wave of nostalgia and nausea both made him break out in sweat and futile conjecture.

He wanted to kill her. She seemed so much like the first source of his own particular anxiety. She had discarded the bobby sox and peter-pan collars, the red lips and heavy tits but the smell was there: the foul cock-teasing odour that aroused to deny in the politics of purity. He knew if he asked her to fuck outright, with no euphemism and no courtesy, with no bullshit, that she would die of the shame. The knowledge gave him a hardon and a sensation of giddy delight.

But she agreed, casually, without guile, and struck him dumb with confusion. She was not what she seemed. And he had been so *sure*.

I'll be damned if I didn't see that weird guy again the very next night. He didn't fuck around I'll give him that. He just said "Could I take you for a beer when you're finished?" and I laughed and said "You sure you won't run away on me?" and he smiled no and was very suave so off we went, me really tongue-tied at first. I liked him, he wasn't so odd as all that given his age which was I believe at least forty. It seems he just wanted me to talk all the time and tell about myself like he was writing a goddamn book or something. He called me Rosa and forever after too even though I said my name. I never found out his as I just called him Professor in fun and it stuck. To this day I don't know what he did exactly as he always said it didn't matter. I do know that when people say such and such doesn't matter it usually does. We really consumed a lot of beer between the two of us. "What do you think of Time?" he asked. "I think they're closing," I said. And he laughed and laughed for I'll bet a full five minutes till I had to pound him on the back, he was choking.

The professor operated from a debilitating perspective of memory and fantasy: thus his preoccupation with Time. Something vital was missing. He felt dreadfully alone and the dread made him seek out Ida. She was not what she seemed. Perhaps nothing was. She'd been an expression of what crippled him, he was sure of that; but something had changed her. There was a chance.

Help me, he prayed to no one in particular.

The truth is I was really flattered to have his attentions. Though I don't see how he could have been interested in my intelligence you know, he never once laid a hand on me either. That just never came up. He'd talk about it sometimes but it was like he was talking about somebody else, it had nothing to do with me. He was a very serious person and would talk about Capital T Truth like you or I'd talk about Shirl's varicose veins. It got really boring in the end and yet I couldn't get him to do nothing else. It drove me crazy but I was flattered all the same.

I once asked him after about ninety beers what it was he liked about me anyway. He smoothed my hair with his big warm hand and said "Rosa girl, I have fallen irrevocably in love with your colossal stupidity." Well I should have been insulted at that but I could tell by his face he meant it to be taken in a good way. I really think he did love me. Hell. I'll bet plenty of people have been loved for worse.

Ida had a survivor's knack for insulating herself against pain. She might deaden the senses with fact or she might just deaden the senses. Despite the yellow curtains she quickly slipped into a smog of comfortable despair and gained 20 pounds in five weeks with an overdose of Dad's chocolate covered oatmeal cookies. Only after her encounter with the professor did she realize the extent of her isolation and long for something different. He had aroused in her an old instinct for wholeness and she understood then that her balance was off.

He thought I could help him. That's what he said finally. He figured I knew something he didn't which is totally dumb as he knew so much about everything. I don't know. I had a lot of respect for his mind and even for his person but he wouldn't *do* anything and that's what got me down. It was all talk. Oh I don't mean screwing and stuff as I can do without that easy. He just wouldn't carry through any of his billion ideas on how he should live or work or anything. He was afraid I guess. Just what anybody's afraid of I have never been able to figure out. A person should be able to have a little fun and kind of get along without worrying so much about what might happen. I told him to piss off once as I couldn't stand it anymore. I couldn't be his friend but he shouldn't have taken it so bad as I couldn't seem to be anybody's friend. I find it easier to fuck and fool around than be a friend. I don't know. It's too bad though that he pissed off for good like that. I got a note.

I DID IT. FUCK YOU ROSA.

What are you saying? What happened?

He drove off a mountain. Do you know Vancouver at all? He drove off the crummy road that goes up to Squamish. Fell into the sea.

How did you feel?

Alright. He'd been good company for a long time so I felt somewhat sad for myself of course but it was probably the only solution for him so I was happy in that. Too bad about the note. It really wrecked everything; it really got me down.

I've never been especially interesting to look at. For one thing my nose is too big and for another my eyes are terribly small but if I do say so myself I've always had real beautiful hair. Thick and full of gold and red. My Dad loved it for one ever since I can remember. With the professor gone there sure wasn't any reason to stick around that cruddy wet place and I felt I just had to get home so bad. But the truth was I had no money saved at all and I mean none. I was making $1.25 an hour but hell by the time I paid out for bus fares and my house and groceries and smokes etcetera I had nothing. So you see I got this idea to cut my hair and sell it. You're always reading about how much they pay for good hair for wigs and whatnot I thought sure I'd get twenty-five or thirty bucks especially as I had so much of it and I'd be able to get a bus back to Alberta. I'd heard too many awful stories about girls hitching to try that.

When I got off work I went home to my little house and got my nail scissors which of course were too small so I had to get the bread knife. Slice slice gold on brown paper, butcher's paper, slice, all my beautiful hair and I couldn't help but cry some I looked so awful and it was like I'd done a wrong thing there. I wished I was dead. I remembered the Samson story and wished I was dead please god please god. I used the nail scissors to trim the ends.

Of course you can't let yourself go can you? What's done's done. By morning I'd worked myself up to looking forward to the trip home again never mind what I looked like. I had a dollar left and got the bus downtown. As per usual it was raining. What's new? God that's depressing. There's an outfit down on Hastings Street that makes wigs up and sells to all the other stores in town.

I got off the bus too soon and had to walk down past the White Lunch cafeteria where all the winos and old men hang out. Boy I hate that. They sit there sucking sugar lumps and staring. It gives me the creeps. They never move. They looked at me and didn't see nothing. I looked right back and wished to god I had a machine gun. By the time I got there all I wanted was to get my money and get moving. This tit receptionist said "Can I help you dear?" but you could see she didn't care for me at all. "I've got some hair to sell," I said. "I'm sorry, we do all our buying in Hong Kong." "It's blond," I said and showed her. She kept looking past me all the time. "It's policy," she said, "I'm sorry." She wasn't. And neither was I. No fuckhead was going to wear my hair. Jesus jesus jesus. I went down to Woolworths and got some jelly doughnuts and coffee. I was soaked through and my nose was running. As if that wasn't enough some real ugly pimply kid in a blue ski jacket sat down and asked me if I wanted to go to Stanley Park. I scared the pants off him by starting to bawl —right there in Woolworths out loud and everything. "I didn't mean nothing," he said and took off. I just cried and cried. My face got all swollen and red and my nose was running. I couldn't breathe but I couldn't stop as I'd never been so terribly unhappy.

*

Some people might say that Lucy was primarily concerned with acting out her own fantasies, with making dream deed. It's a nice thought but the premise is false; Lucy never had a fantasy in her life. She nearly died once for the lack of it.

On a dry afternoon in August '71 Lucy boarded a Greyhound in Cadillac Sask. knowing neither where she'd been nor where she was heading. Movement itself sufficed for Lucy. But the hot dry day burned through the tinted glass and scorched her skin. The clear pleasure of journey was lost. She did not sweat. Head to toe she felt the skin grow brittle and crack but she could not sweat and the cold in her bones was dreadful. 'Better die than lie' she recited but the words rang hollow. She stretched out one thin hand to pull the shade and saw no hand at all but an odd transparent likeness, all form and no substance. Even that frail image faded into hot white glare when the bus lurched to a stop. Her panic was immense but when the bus moved on again that too subsided. Someone was sitting next to her. Ida, she thought. The glare dimmed to a thin white line and Lucy slept.

When she awoke it was dark. She was wet with sweat, cool and rested. On the seat next to her lay an empty book of matches where neatly inscribed in her own handwriting she read:

> Ha! Better lie than die.
> We are all jews.
> We are all jews.
> I am a jew.

Very occasionally one has flashes of clarity when the will is exposed for the raw remorseless thing that it is. In an instant it sees both time and space as a sham, but the will is quick to obscure its godliness in the interests of preservation. Another moment and the same white light burns out the credibility of the will itself. The flesh survives.

All I could think was to get home out of the rain and low sky back to the prairie. I couldn't breathe and I put it down to there being no space in the air I could see. I never even went back to my little house or anything. I asked two people the way but they just looked at me funny so I went into Eatons and looked at an atlas and figured out the road I wanted and how to get there. I'm very coolheaded when it comes to that. I spent my last quarter taking the bus out to Boundary Road and walked up to where the Grandview Highway ran into the freeway. I was freezing cold but my head was clear and in twenty minutes I got a ride as far as Hope. It seemed I was meeting a lot of pimply types that day. This one had a stereo tape deck but if anything he was more of a loser than ski jacket in that he didn't even have the gumption to make a pass though you could see he was aching to. He blushed when I asked for a cigarette for Chrissake and gave me the whole pack so I wouldn't have to ask again I guess. He drove like a maniac all the way too—showing off like. I can never feel sorry for guys like that either. It's like they put all their effort into being creeps. They really make me puke. He pulled into a Royalite when we got there and I asked him for a dollar. You could see he was cheap and didn't want to give it but it didn't fit with his big-mover image so he gave me two in fact. After a couple of O Henrys I tried hitching again but nobody stopped so I went into the cafe for some chips and coffee smoking like a chimney. I was feeling pretty good and even threw away a quarter on the jukebox. Outside again it was awful. Hope is probably the most depressing place in the world stuck right in the mountains like that. It makes you feel like giving up. But I wasn't out there long when an old guy in a pickup pulled over. He was going up by Williams Lake somewhere and I felt real safe as soon as I got in. He didn't say nothing, he was like my Dad, and I offered him a smoke but he said no that he just chewed the stuff. I felt so good I fell right asleep till he poked me and said "You going east?" "Yeah. Alberta!" "Better get out here then." I knew by the look of things we were in Cache Creek. "Thanks," I said. He just gave me a neat little nod and pulled out.

Well I still felt sort of the shits but there's actually some sky in Cache Creek you know. With all that sky I had to stand around for ages just breathing in and out. It was getting dark but who cares? Things were looking up. I even had $1.30 left so I got smokes and went into the hotel there, the Oasis would you believe, for a sandwich.

I waited a helluva time for a ride. At ten some guy stopped in a little Corvair or something. I wasn't even sat down when he said "I'll tell you now I don't have any money worth stealing." I wanted to tell him that all money's worth stealing but he looked so serious I let my mouth fall open instead. He smiled then and said "Well you never know" which I guess is true enough. Unlike the others he was a regular chatterbox. I knew his whole life story practically by the time we passed through Kamloops. I guess he was nervous with me there. He was going to Edmonton to pick up his wife and kids and bring them back home to Chilliwack. It wasn't anything heavy though, they'd just been on holidays or something. I don't know. From the general picture I got of his life I figured I was the first woman he'd been with in such close quarters excepting his wife for maybe fifteen years. It was very odd. He calmed down after about three hundred miles—once he realized I wasn't one of those women in *Argosy* I guess.

If you want to hear something really funny I'll tell you the truth. That was the best night of my life. Here was this total tit—an accountant or something—and me, Ida Johnson, barrelling over the Rockies in a tinny crud car and it's the best memory I've got. The idea was to stay awake. We found out we knew a lot of the same songs and sang and sang and yelled out the windows. I told him things I never even knew I knew about and vice versa. I was never so close to being me. It's because that was all I guess. It didn't matter what he thought as I'd never see him again. It didn't even matter that we'd probably hate each other in real life. We had breakfast in Banff and got to Calgary just past nine. He let me off on the Macleod Trail and we shook hands and said "Good Luck." It was very nice.

It took me the whole bloody day to get home to Longview. Since it was dark and there still weren't any street lights in the old place I couldn't see the house. It took a while to get it through my skull there wasn't any house. There was nothing but a black pile of rubble. I started yelling "Ole! Ole!" and the next thing I knew I was in Yvonne's kitchen drinking rye and she was talking a mile a minute: "...we tried getting hold of you Ida but nobody seemed to know where exactly though we got in contact with the Mounties and everything but we couldn't find you. It's been two months, must've been a leak, your Mom inside and dear me yes Ole was alright I saw him in the yard, watched him walk in just walk right in, after her I guess I don't know it was so awful, I'm sorry, Bob and the Miller boys got him out but there was no use, I tried, he said, over and over I don't know what he meant but to get Esther I guess I'm sorry, I'm sorry..." My crying wasn't for Ole but for me left there; who would I go home to now? I saw the funny side of it alright but I couldn't help my crying any the less. I could've told him he was too old. I should've said something. What the hell? What could I have said? I asked Yvonne if I could stay the night and she said "Of course" and that she'd run me up to Chuck's in the morning but I said "No" as we didn't really have any connection but then I remembered I had no money or anything so I said "Yeah. Thanks" and slept like a log on the rollaway in the kitchen I was so tired after the trip. In the morning I went out to check on the situation but there was really nothing. As it seemed sure I'd never get back I went down and sat in the gully awhile not thinking of anything just sitting there trying to get the feel of things more or less. Bob gave me a deck of Players before he went to work and said about being sorry. Not a bad guy, Bob.

I did four days' worth of dishes for Yvonne, she always was a pig housekeeper, and then we took off for Turner Valley dropping the kids at school. They've got this big modern school there now and the one I went to was all overgrown with grass and shit. She had the radio on so we didn't have to say anything. Chuck was real nice too and put his arms around me though he'd never done such a thing before. He'd really gotten old and depressing though and I knew right off I couldn't stay more than I had to. He was doing alright moneywise working for Home Oil and was even going to night school in Calgary once a week "to improve myself" as he put it. Cheryl was working part-time in the hardware store with the kids all at school now. He was doing okay but somehow I liked him better when he had his trap line and if I do say so myself I think he liked himself more then too. "What happened to your hair?" he asked. "It's a long story," I said. "It'll grow." It wasn't all great. He told me I looked awful for instance and said it was time I straightened up. Wanted me to improve myself I guess. He told me I'd been an asshole to Mom etcetera which in retrospect was true but hell, all that was over now wasn't it? I told him about the fix I was in and he gave me fifty bucks just like that. I went out and got a *Western Producer* at the drugstore. Chuck had to go to work at four so I had to spend the evening alone with Cheryl but we watched TV a lot so it wasn't bad. I was going to write letters to a bunch of ads but the thought of hanging around there waiting for an answer turned me right off so I more or less closed my eyes and ran my finger down the column and where it stopped I'd go. That's it. The end. It was Shirl's Claresholm ad I stopped at. Chuck took me into Calgary in the morning and bought my bus ticket on top of the fifty and everything. I guess he was glad I was getting on my way too. "I'm sorry," he said. "What the hell," I said. I been waiting around here ever since. Just waiting.

*

Ida is sitting perfectly still. Her head is clear. Luke feels drained. They regard each other from a great distance for an interminable length of time. At last Luke closes the gap. With one long haunting look he lets go the illusion of the space between. He comes home.

"Lucy," says Ida, utterly calm, "you took your fucking time."

Lucy's hand shakes so bad she can no longer hold her cup. It makes no sense at all this coming here, she thinks. But then neither did that yo-yo act of running off somewhere only to remain a miscast shadow. No. The sense of it lay in a humour much broader than her own. She hopes that Ida will take her close and hold her. Please, she thinks, please. Ida's stare stops her cold.

"Come on," she says, "I got my own place over the garage. First I want my twenty bucks. Jesus H."

Lucy follows Ida out of the cafe, across to the garage, up a dreary none-too-clean stairway. The door to Ida's room is painted bright prime yellow; she explains it away as an attempt to put some colour in her life.

Lucy says, "I think it's nice," and means it.

Ida undoes the two padlocks and pulls open the door. "You're the first person I ever had in here," she says.

The room is surreal. It gives a startling sense of order and incredible beauty. Everything fits but Ida and yet it has come from her. Lucy feels disoriented and foolish. She knows nothing. It reflects à mind so finely drawn and self-possessed, so lacking in *ressentiment*, that it seems, somehow, inhuman. Its very perfection provides the Final Solution. None but the holy could live in a room like this; none but the whole. The terrible strength of it would eat them alive.

"I've got my own bathroom," she says, pointing proudly across the room to an identical yellow door. "This is my home."

*

Lucy was an old soul. She'd been born out of the grave with her sense of past intact and an immortal's disregard for the particulars of time and place. She understood the inconsequence of all things and acted accordingly; experience was as illusory as dream. (In point of fact she even got married once—or was it twice?) Her needs and habits were human; her peculiarity lay in her ability to see without shadow. She understood it was all for nothing and occasionally, in consequence, that it was all for everything. Her strength was her self. "I am the beginning and the end." It was also her downfall. That and the distance that grew without pause between her and the world.

It was Ida who first made her aware of both disparities. Stupid little Ida with the big teeth and thick braids. "Right as rain," she'd say or "God's truth!" She believed everything. Lucy told her the truth once. They'd made a snow fort in the gully. The day was hard and white, framed in ice. Ida's mute stoicism had long both puzzled and annoyed Lucy. She was intrigued to the point of doing herself harm. The sun bit into her brain; in one stupid moment she exposed herself irrevocably, hoping Ida would give some clue in return. "Ida," she said, "we can do anything. There's nothing to stop us. Nothing you see here is real. We're making it up. I tell you we can make up anything." Ida sat down on the snow stool she'd just made to think about it. "You mean," she asked, "all this snow here isn't really snow at all?" "It's only an idea," said Lucy. "Whose?" she asked like an idiot. "Ours!" yelled Lucy. "Whose idea are we then?" Lucy hit her. The question was absurd. There was a will to life and that's all. A greedy sucking urge to become. But the disintegration had begun. Ida was right. If the world was false then perhaps so too was the will: an idea and nothing more. There were no half measures. The centre lost its hold. She was a fool. It didn't bear thinking about, was Ida's opinion.

Lucy's fear of her own dissolution made the previously acceptable distancing of herself from the world unbearable. As long as she danced solid in contradiction to illusion her isolation seemed natural. If her dance was equally false where lay the sense? She wanted somebody to help her, to be and believe with; somebody to obscure her sight with shadow. The only one with enough strength was Ida. All these years and all those people later and the only one who could save her broken drive was the very reason it lay in pieces. No, none of it bore thinking about.

*

Lucy's face dulls to a ghostly pallor; her eyes dim in the fine light. She slumps on Ida's colourful bed in Ida's colourful room and begins to cry—the low keen of an animal consoling itself from fear or fatigue.

"Jesus, what's the matter?" asks Ida with feigned interest.

There is no response. Lucy has never lost a tear in her life but there's no stopping it now. Ida lights a Players and lets her weep. It's none of my affair, she thinks. But her slow smile seems oddly timed and indicates that perhaps it is. The thought, like the question, comes out of habit. In fact she feels a release of exhileration: she's come back into her own.

All through the long afternoon Lucy weeps and Ida sits watch. By nightfall it is over. The noise stops as abruptly as it began. Ida stands at the window looking out to the highway. Lucy smiles stupidly in her direction: what she'd lost in vision she's gained in tired peace. She feels she could lay there forever. It is the repose of the dead.

Ida stares resolutely out into the dark. Her features are blurred from where Lucy lay but her heavy silhouette is as comforting as memory. She speaks quietly and to the point without turning or shifting her gaze. "You were too long coming back. It's pure luck that I'm here at all. I lost touch more times than I can count."

"I'm sorry," Lucy says, but thinks nothing. "I had a few problems myself."

Ida doesn't hear. She is listening for something else. "We've got to get going," she says. "It's time I was on the move again."

Lucy rises from the bed to lay a damp kiss on the back of Ida's neck. "I'm real tired," she says. "Can't it wait till morning?"

A coyote calls out across the prairie. Ida turns from the window grinning like crazy. "I'll carry you awhile now," she says. Lucy takes hold of her outstretched arm and together they walk out and down to the highway.

"Was all that stuff back there true?" asks Lucy.

Ida laughs. "What's the matter sweetheart? You miss the point or something?"

*